Contents

Our senses

Our senses tell us about the world.

We use our sense of sight to see things.

We use our sense of hearing to hear things.

We use our sense of smell to smell things.

Ways into Science

Senses

Written by Peter Riley

W

FRANKLIN WATTS

LONDON • SYDNEY

First published in 2003 by Franklin Watts
96 Leonard Street, London EC2A 4XD

Franklin Watts Australia
45-51 Huntley Street
Alexandria, NSW 2015

Series editor: Sarah Peutrill
Art director: Jonathan Hair
Design: Ian Thompson
Photography: Ray Moller (unless otherwise
credited)

A CIP catalogue record for this book is
available from the British Library

ISBN 0 7496 4733 7

Printed in Hong Kong/China

Picture Credits:
Bruce Coleman Inc p. 8b; Paul Doyle/Photofusion p. 13t;
Robert Pickett/Papilio p. 17b

Thanks to our models:
Amber Barkhouse, Reece Calvert, Shani-e Cox,
Chantelle Daniel, Ammar Duffus, Alex Green,
Harry Johal and Emily Scott

To my granddaughter Megan Kate

We use our
sense of
taste to
taste things.

We use our sense of
touch to feel things.

What can
you sense
right now?

Sight

Our eyes give us our sense of sight.

Your eyes can only see what is in front of you.

A chameleon can turn its eyes in different directions so it can see all round.

8

We can see different colours. How many colours can you see on Ben's T-shirt?

We can see things that are near.

We can also see things that are far away.

Look out of a window. What is the furthest thing you can see?

9

We see things when light goes into our eyes. It goes through a hole called a pupil.

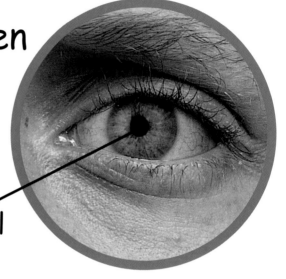

Pupil

Our pupils can change size. When it is bright our pupils are smaller.

Hannah is in bright light. Her pupils are small.

When it is darker, our pupils grow larger so they let in more light to help us see.

Hannah sits in a shady place. Her pupils have become large.

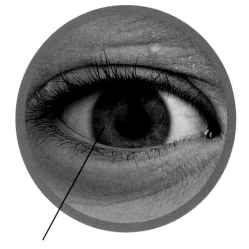

This is a brown iris.

The iris is the coloured ring around the pupil. It has muscles that make the pupil change size.

What colour are your irises?

Hearing

Our ears give us our sense of hearing.

We can hear sounds all around us.

Tom can hear music on his headphones.

Katie can hear a door closing behind her.

We can hear loud sounds clearly.

Loud sounds can hurt our ears. People who work in very noisy places wear ear protectors.

Quiet sounds, like rustling leaves, can be difficult to hear.

Sally puts her hand round her ear. What do you think happens? Turn the page to find out.

13

Hearing test

Sally can hear the leaves rustling more clearly. Try cupping your hands around your ears to hear a noise better.

Here is another hearing game.

Raj sits on a chair and puts on a blindfold.

Laura has two coins.

14

Laura stands near Raj. She clicks the coins together.

Raj points to where he thinks Laura is.

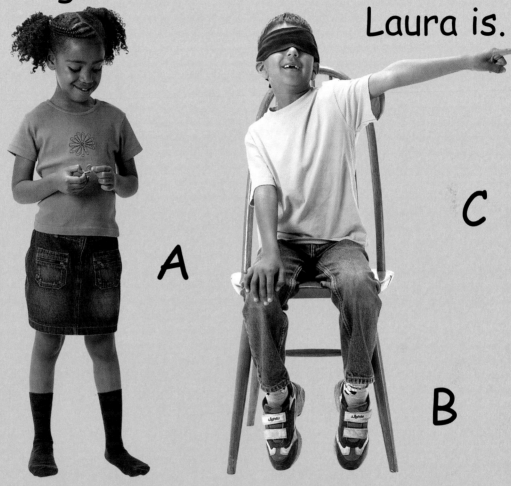

A

C

B

Laura moves to place A, B and C and clicks the coins each time. Raj gets better at guessing where she is.

Try Laura's test on your friends.

Smell

Our nose gives us our sense of smell.

All sorts of things can be smelled.

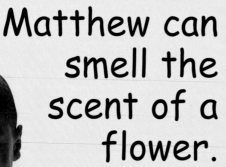

Matthew can smell the scent of a flower.

16

Hannah can smell shoe polish.

Some smells
are pleasant.

Some smells are
unpleasant.

Dogs need a
better sense
of smell than
humans. Can
you think why?

Smell test

Sam has some clean, empty yogurt pots.

He puts a different piece of food in each one.

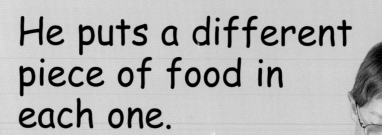

Sam covers each pot with kitchen towel.

Sam gives a yogurt pot to Nicole.

Nicole sniffs the top of the pot.

She uses her sense of smell to guess what the food is.

Nicole tries all the pots.

Is it onion?

Try Sam's test on your friends.

Taste

Our tongue gives us our sense of taste. We use it to tell us about our food and drinks.

Everyone has a different sense of taste.

Laura likes strawberries.

Raj does not.

Our tongues can tell four different tastes. These are: sweet, salty, sour and bitter.

Paul has some foods with different tastes.

Which taste do you think each one has?

vinegar

jam

sweets

coffee

bacon

lemon

salted crisps

Find out on the next page.

Four tastes

Sour

Bitter

Sweet

Salty

Did you sort the foods like Paul?

Taste test

Hannah holds her nose
and chews an apple.

She cannot taste
the apple well.

Hannah lets go of her nose.

She can taste the apple now.

Try the test with an adult.

Touch

Our skin gives us our sense of touch.

We can feel a hard floor with our bare feet.

We can feel the softness of a pillow with our face.

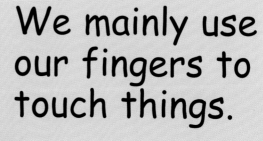

We mainly use our fingers to touch things.

Things can
feel rough
or smooth.

 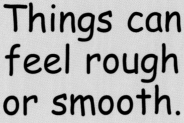

Sandpaper
feels rough.

An apple skin
feels smooth.

Things can
feel warm
or cold.

This cup feels
warm.

This glass
feels cold.

Touch test

Raj puts an apple in a bag. He gives the bag to Katie.

Katie feels in the bag.

Katie guesses what the object is. She checks to see if she is right.

Try this test on your friends.

Using your senses

We use our senses all the time. We often use them together.

Make a table like this one. Put a tick next to the senses you use.

Activity	Sight	Hearing	Smell	Taste	Touch
Cross a road					
Play on a computer					
Enjoy a meal					
Play catch					

Think of some other activities. Add them to your table.

Useful words

bright – when the light that reaches your eyes is very strong.

far – something that is a long way away.

hearing – the sense that tells us how something sounds.

iris – a ring of colour in the eye that makes the pupil bigger or smaller.

muscle – one of the parts inside the body that makes movement.

near – something that is close by.

pupil – the hole in the middle of the eye.

rough – something that is uncomfortable to touch because it has lumps and uneven parts.

sense – one of the five things that tell us about the world around us. The five senses are touch, taste, sight, hearing and smell.

shade – somewhere where there is not much light.

sight – the ability to see things with your eyes.

smell – the ability to sense things with your nose.

soft – something that is gentle to touch.

taste – the sense you use to tell you what something you are eating or drinking is like.

touch – the sense you use to feel things and know what they are like.

Some answers

Here are some answers to some of the questions we have asked in this book. Don't worry if you had some different answers to ours; you may be right, too. Talk through your answers with other people and see if you can explain why they are right.

Page 7 You are probably using your sense of sight to see things such as the page in the book. You may be using your sense of hearing to hear things around you. If you think about it you will use your sense of touch to feel the pages of the book and the clothes on your skin.

Page 9 Ben's shirt has five colours (yellow, blue, orange, black and white). We can't tell you how far you can see. Perhaps it is just across the street or a hill a long way off.

Page 11 Your irises may be blue, brown, grey-blue or green.

Page 17 Dogs need a stronger sense of smell to find food.

Page 27 You may have put ticks in the table to show that – when you cross a road you use your sense of sight and hearing; when you play on the computer you use your sense of sight, sense of hearing and sense of touch; when you enjoy a meal you use your sense of sight, sense of smell and sense of taste; when you play catch you use your sense of sight and your sense of touch.

Index

About this book

Ways into Science is designed to encourage children to begin to think about their everyday world in a scientific way, examining cause and effect through close observation, recording their results and discussing what they have seen. Here are some pointers to gain maximum use from **Senses**.

• Working through this book will introduce the basic concepts of the senses and also some of the vocabulary associated with them. This will prepare the child for more formal work later in the school curriculum.

• On pages 13 and 21 the children are invited to predict the results of a particular action or test. Ensure that you discuss the reason for any answer they give in some depth before turning over the page. In answering the question on page 13 look for an answer that mentions how the hand makes the ear larger to catch sounds. In answering the question on page 21 discuss the foods with the children and ask them to remember how they tasted.

• Throughout the use of the book encourage the children to think about all their senses, for example even when they are reading about light in the eye you may like to ask them what can they hear, feel or even smell.

• The question on page 11 about the colour of irises can be extended to a class survey and used as an example of how people vary in their features.

• You may like to extend the work on sight on pages 8 – 11 by using **Light and Dark**, another title in the Ways into Science series.

• You may like to extend the work on hearing on pages 12 – 15 by using **Sound**, another title in the Ways into Science series.